Flowers in Season

See page 49.

2 *See page 50.*

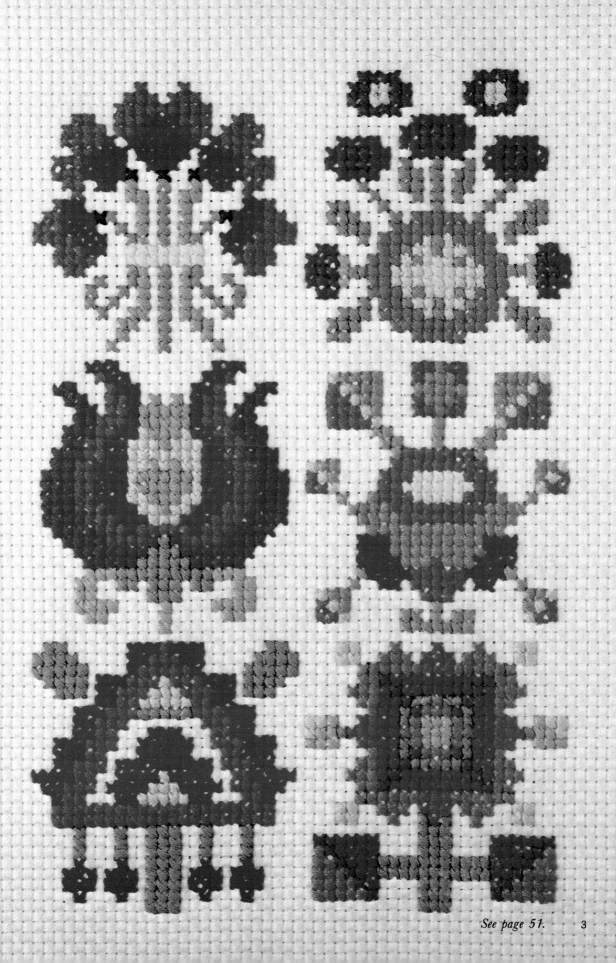

See page 51.

See page 52.

See page 53.   5

6   *See page 54.*

See page 55.

8   *See page 56.*

See page 57.

10   *See page 58.*

See page 59.

See page 60 · 61.

Merry-Go-Round

See page 62.

See page 63. 15

See page 64.

See page 65.

See page 66 · 67.

20　　*See page 68.*

See page 69.

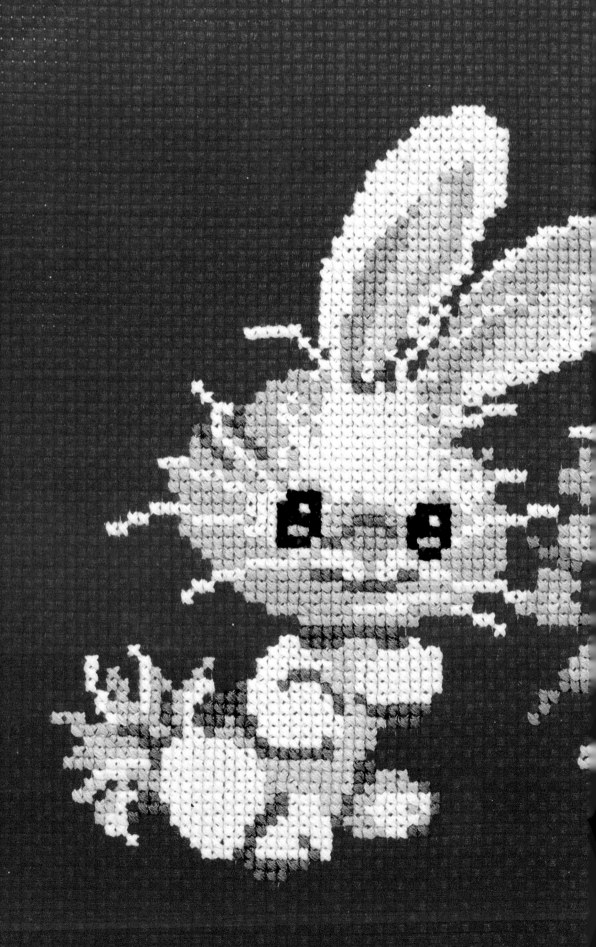

See page 70 · 71.

24 *See page 72.*

See page 73.

See page 74 · 75.

For Wall Frames

See page 76.

See page 77.

30   *See page 78.*

See page 79.

See page 80.

See page 83.

See page 84.

Geometric Patterns

See page 86.

See page 87.

See page 82.

See page 81.

Monograms

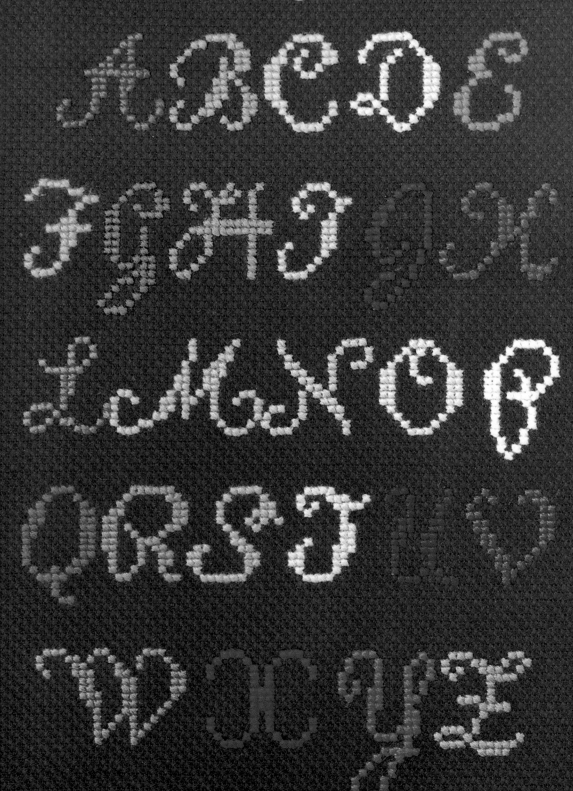

See page 88.

See page 89.

Kitchenette Items

See page 90.

See page 91.

Linked Motifs

See page 92.

See page 93.

See page 94.

See page 95.   47

48   *See page 96.*

◯=602	⟋=603	◣=605	●=309	✳=335	✕=3326	•=818
▲=947	⬗=973	◎=741	◤=725	▽=727	T=743	V=971
⟩=742	◐=783	✕=3045	☐=3045(HOLBEIN)	◥=976	A=977	⬚=915
☐=915(HOLBEIN)	≡=917	⊥=718	⌐=605	◉=327	◥=553	∩=554
△=702	☐=702(HOLBEIN)	⬭=913	✕=911	‖=988	∅=3347	✕=3346
⟨=910	✳=991	⊞=3012	‖=320	✢=471	⬙=797	
⬙=797(HOLBEIN)	✚=826	⟋=813	✕=519	⬚=519(HOLBEIN)	⊟=791	■=310
					◻=WHITE	

49

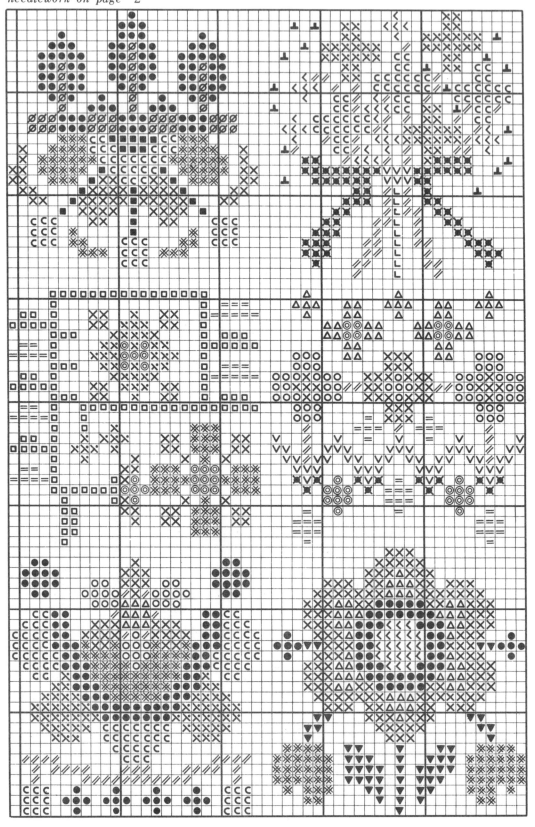

⊠ =892 ● =606 ✕ =601 ⊙ =603 ⊂ =947 ✖ =971 ∅ =321 ⟨ =742 ⊥ =307 △ =208 ▫ =700

▼ =701 ═ =702 ◎ =704 ∥ =943 L =993 V =995 ✱ =996 ■ =823

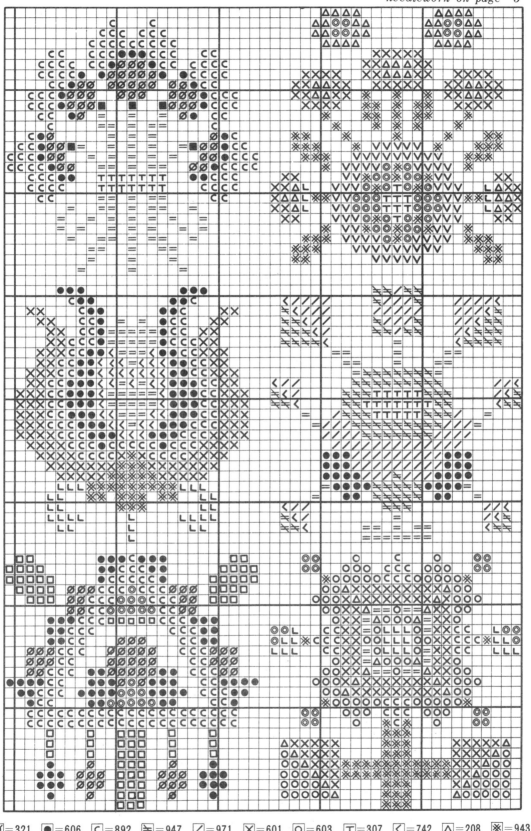

Ø=321 ●=606 C=892 ✕=947 ∕=971 ✕=601 O=603 T=307 ≺=742 △=208 ✳=943

□=700 ═=702 ◎=704 L=993 V=995 ■=823

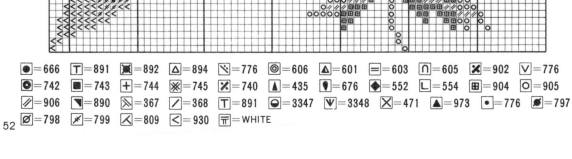

◯ =604	△=602	⧄=601	▫=603	◕=498	⊞=666	⧈=608	⊔=891	⌴=891(HOLBEIN)	⬈=892
⤬=894	ǀ=818	⊏=744	⌴=744(HOLBEIN)	✳=435	■=838	▨=434	⊞=915	▲=917	↓=918
⌗=550	⟙=552	∠=553	⁂=211	◕=987	●=3345	✕=3346	◉=3348	◆=986	△=987	⸪=988
⋂=320	⊘=906	⊥=702	÷=909	▣=912	⤨=471	⁄=703	⬊=700	▯=895	⊙=797	▼=799
⬒=798	⊤=809	·=800

53

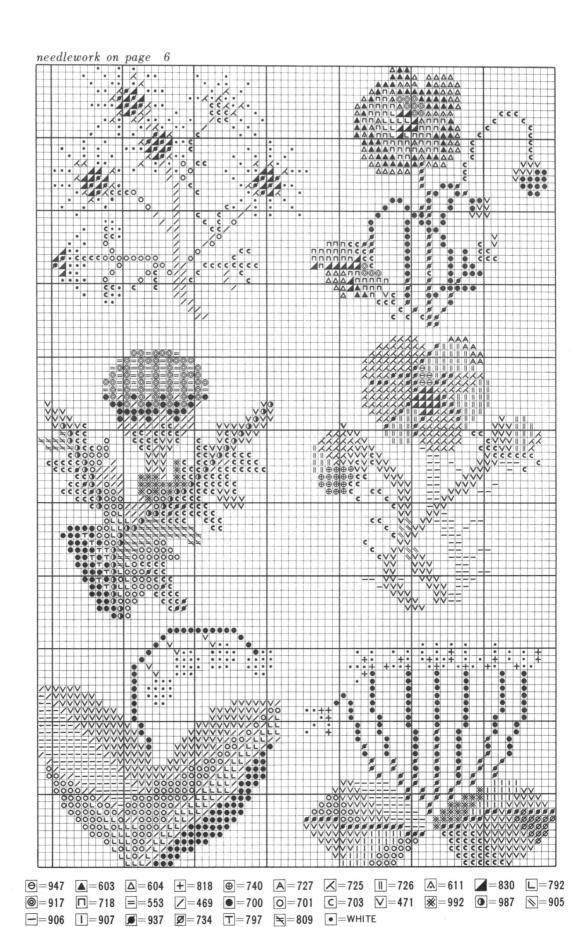

⊖	=947	▲	=603	△	=604	+	=818	⊕	=740	A	=727	⋌	=725	‖	=726	⧄	=611	◢	=830	L	=792
◎	=917	⊓	=718	=	=553	∕	=469	●	=700	O	=701	C	=703	V	=471	※	=992	◑	=987	◹	=905
—	=906	I	=907	◮	=937	∅	=734	T	=797	⋊	=809	•	=WHITE

☐=602	⊞=603	Φ=605	‖=947	▲=725	⊔=741	⊤=822	※=676	═=554	◎=210	⋊=553
C=704	◤=830	☒=831	◪=470	●=699	O=701	⟨=702	╱=703	V=993	◑=996	⊠=907
L=798	•=WHITE									

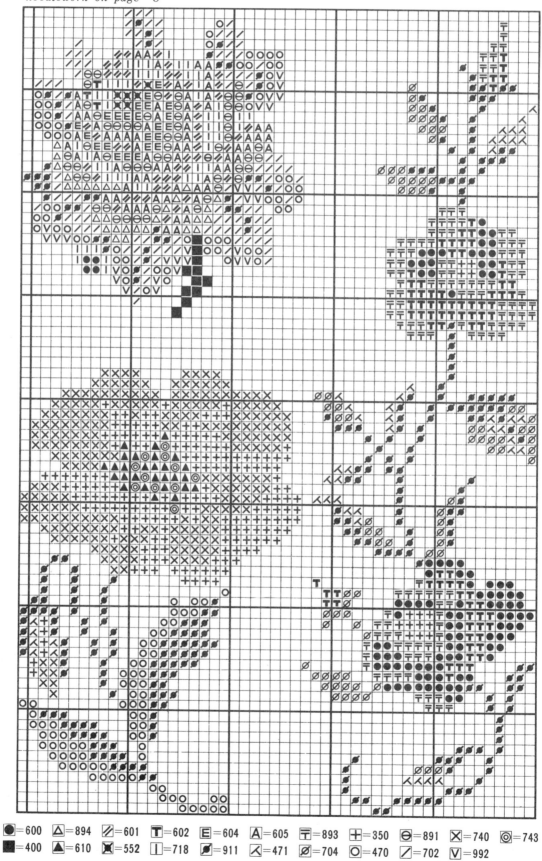

●=600 △=894 ⬰=601 T̄=602 Ē=604 Ā=605 T̅=893 ✚=350 ⊖=891 ☒=740 ◎=743
■=400 ▲=610 ⊠=552 Ī=718 ⬰=911 ⅄=471 ∅=704 O=470 ⬰=702 V=992

‖ =351	◐=600	T =601	✕=604	∅=3328	⊖=892	◎=893	●=326	•=726	A =741	△=740
⁄ =977	■=400	✖=917	─=553	◣=909	⊠=702	○=470	➕=704	V =992	╱=471	⊠=825
⬰=799	L =996	≡=519								

△=352　∠=900　○=321　◉=307　●=783　⫽=552　☰=718　Ⅴ=553　ㄥ=913　✕=907　✖=904
Ⴑ=320　▲=307　L=793

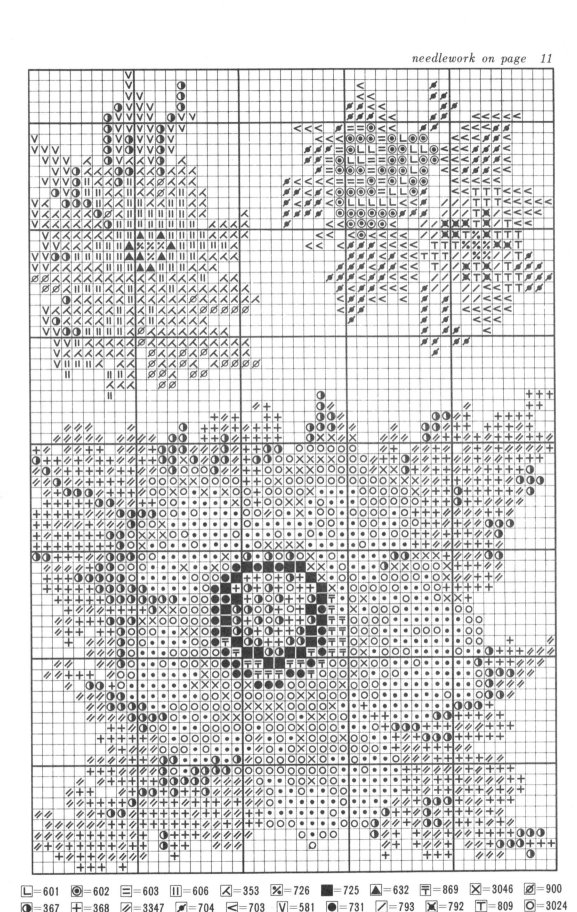

L = 601   ◉ = 602   ≡ = 603   ‖ = 606   ⼈ = 353   ⅗ = 726   ■ = 725   ▲ = 632   〒 = 869   ⊠ = 3046   ∅ = 900

◑ = 367   ✚ = 368   ⫽ = 3347   ⬦ = 704   ⪡ = 703   V = 581   ● = 731   ⁄ = 793   ⊠ = 792   T = 809   ○ = 3024

• = WHITE

■=816　●=814　◖=3350　◉=309　Φ=899　◎=3354　C=3689　O=776　•=963　✖=304　∧=326
Y=761　◪=900　T=350　ɯ=893　◪=3685　ᛕ=891　►=977　←=355　U=758　7=400　◆=552
D=553　◆=554

☑=367 ☒=320 ⊟=368 ▲=895 ⊞=904 ⧄=3346 △=909 ☑=987 ‖=701 ⊟=469 ⊠=935

Ⓛ=905 ✦=319 ◢=3348 ⅼ=3022

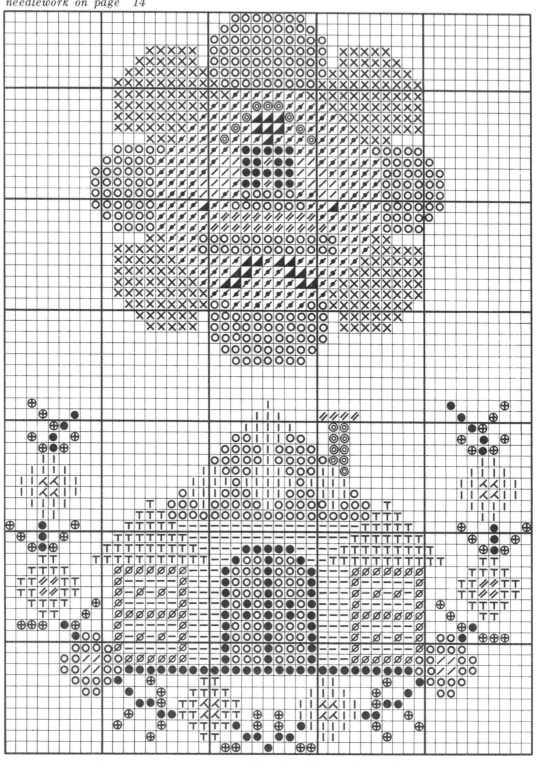

Ⓞ=350 Ⓣ=892 ☒=603 Ⓘ=604 ◤=742 ⊟=642 ⫽=718 ◎=208 ☒=211 ⁄=993 ●=700
⊕=906 Ø=834 ▨=470

O = 350 X = 602 L = 604 T = 892 — = 947 \ = 743 I = 971 ⊕ = 742 ∥ = 718 ◎ = 208 ⅄ = 211
⬛ = 701 ● = 702 △ = 703 ✳ = 907 ▲ = 992 ◐ = 830

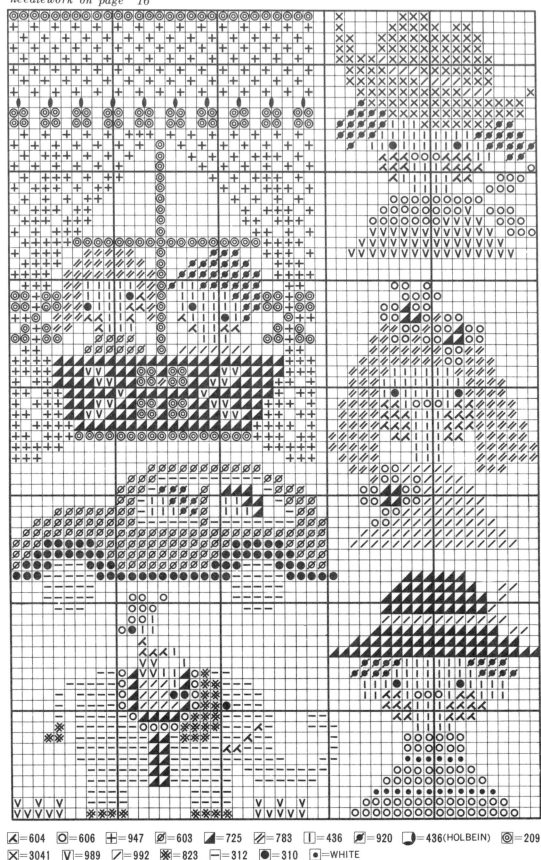

☑=604   ◎=606   ⊞=947   ∅=603   ◢=725   ⊘=783   ☐=436   ⬗=920   ⏝=436(HOLBEIN)   ◎=209

☒=3041   Ⅴ=989   ◿=992   ✳=823   ▭=312   ●=310   ⊙=WHITE

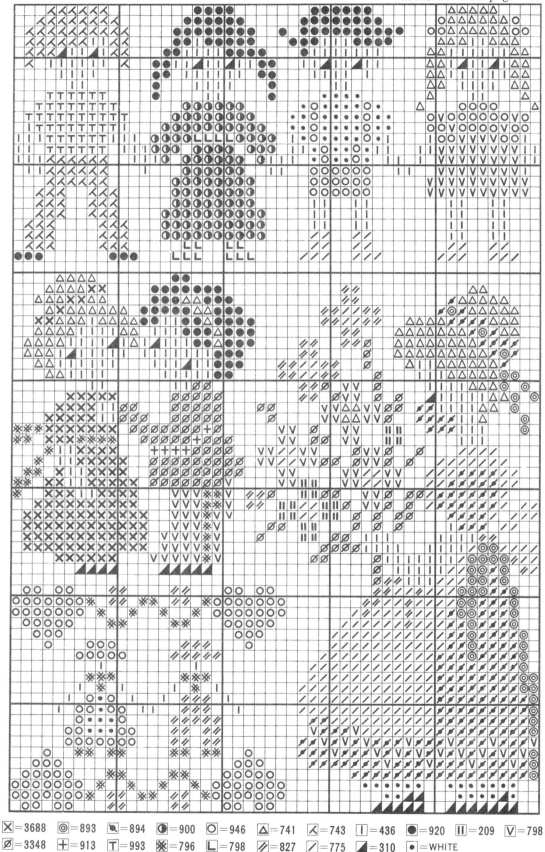

⊠=3688	◎=893	◨=894	◖=900	○=946	△=741	⋋=743	⊺=436	●=920	‖=209	∨=798
⌀=3348	╋=913	⊤=993	✳=796	⌃=798	∥=827	╱=775	◢=310	⊡=WHITE		

●=304 ✕=666 O=818 △=725 V=437 ▲=783 ╱=912 S=367 ╋=472 Ø=3325 ∥=825

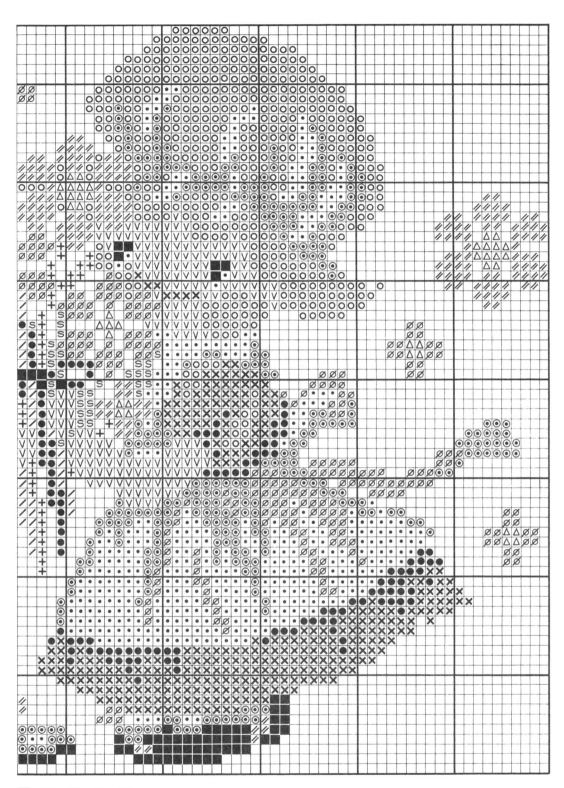

⊙ = 318   ■ = 310   · = WHITE

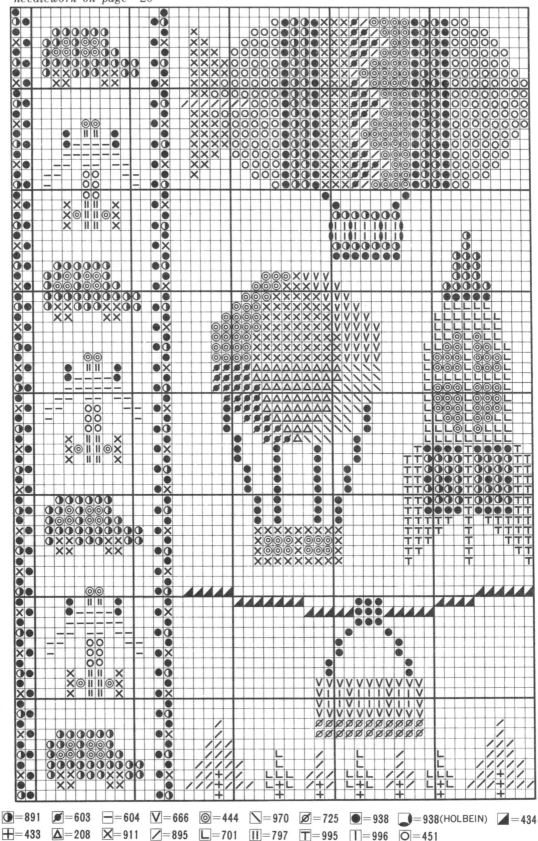

| ◑ =891 | ⬗ =603 | ⊟ =604 | Ⅴ =666 | ◎ =444 | ◥ =970 | ⬙ =725 | ● =938 | ◗ =938(HOLBEIN) | ◢ =434 |
| ⊞ =433 | △ =208 | ⊠ =911 | ⟋ =895 | L =701 | ‖ =797 | T =995 | | =996 | O =451 | |

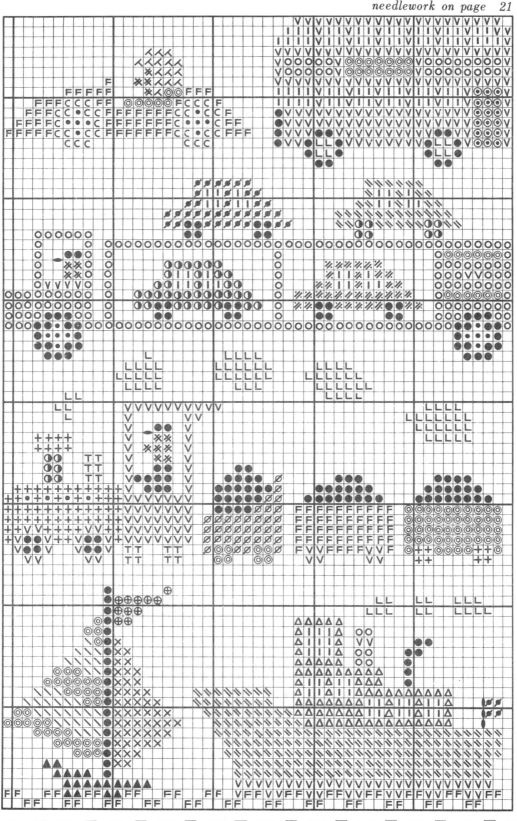

☒=604 ⊿=601 ⊘=603 ⊻=666 ⊗=309 ⊕=351 ⊚=444 ◑=725 ⟍=970 ◎=632 ⊤=841
▲=434 △=977 ●=938 ⬤=938(HOLBEIN) ⊘=208 ◯=701 ✛=991 ☒=911 ⊞=995 ⊺=996
C=311 ⟍=820 ⌶=318 •=WHITE

○=956 ◎=818 ▲=743 ●=610 ◉=738

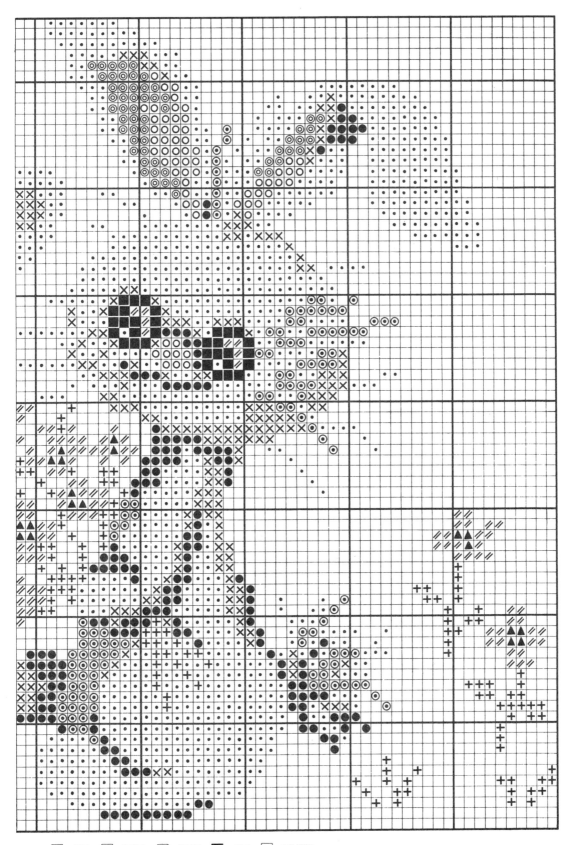

✚=701 ⊘=3325 ☒=3023 ■=310 ⊙=WHITE

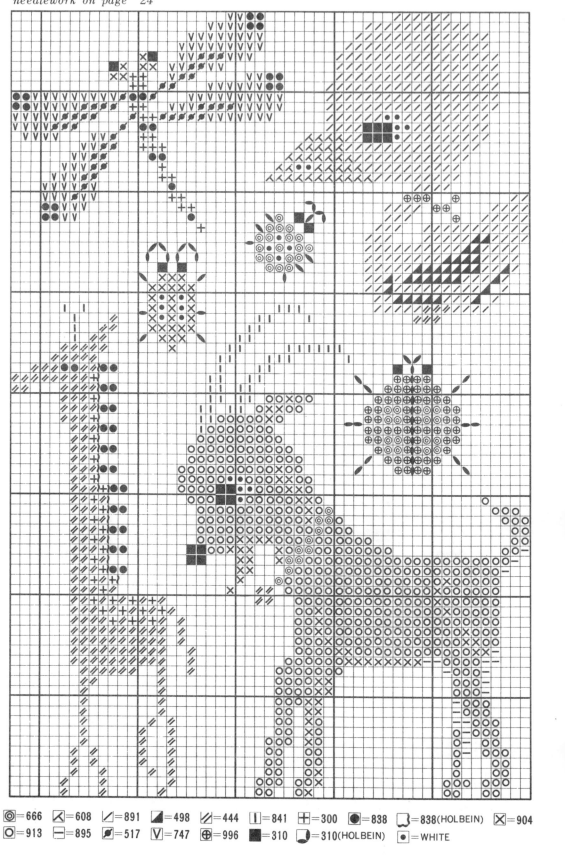

⊚=666 ⟨=608 ⟋=891 ◤=498 ⟋⟋=444 ▯=841 ⊞=300 ⬤=838 ⟋=838(HOLBEIN) ✕=904

◯=913 ⊟=895 ⬗=517 ⱽ=747 ⊕=996 ■=310 ⟋=310(HOLBEIN) ⦿=WHITE

$\boxed{V}$=754	$\boxtimes$=351	$\varnothing$=608	$\boxed{X}$=894	$\boxed{/}$=894(HALF CROSS)	$\circledcirc$=666	$\bigcirc$=666(HOLBEIN)	$\boxed{/\!/}$=444	$\boxed{I}$=841
$\blacktriangle$=838	$\boxed{\blacktriangle\!\!\blacktriangle}$=840	$\boxed{\circ\!\!\mid}$=907	$+$=904	$\mathscr{O}$=935	$\boxed{O}$=996	$\bullet$=995	$-$=517	$\boxed{\blacktriangle}$=311	$\blacksquare$=310	$\bullet$=WHITE

73

$\boxed{\Lambda}$=947　$\boxed{/\!\!/}$=601　$\boxed{/}$=335　$\boxed{2}$=956　$\boxed{I}$=894　$\boxed{\bullet}$=304　$\boxed{\square}$=606　$\boxed{\overline{T}}$=971　$\boxed{\ell}$=972　$\boxed{II}$=973　$\boxed{X}$=838

$\boxed{X\!\!\!X}$=3045　$\boxed{\oplus}$=553　$\boxed{+}$=210　$\boxed{\mathbb{O}}$=917

○ =988　▲=943　△=992　人=907　L=702　S=913　◎=791　•=799　Ø=995　Ø=996

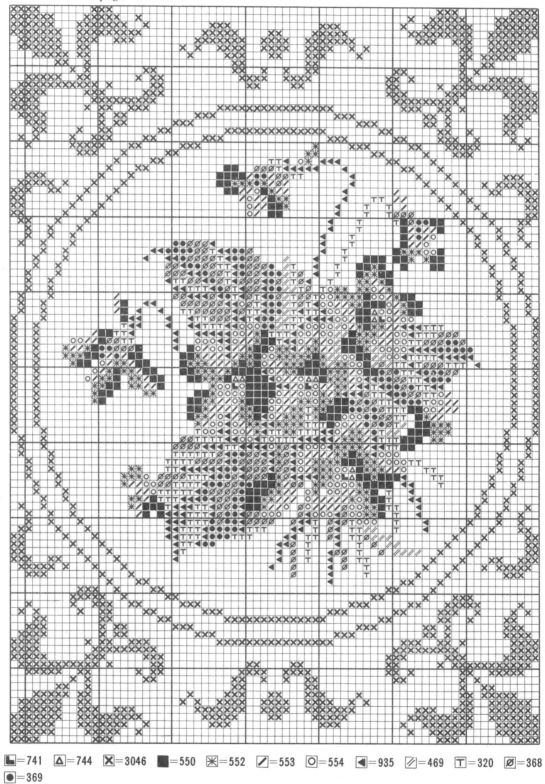

■=741 △=744 ✕=3046 ■=550 ✳=552 ╱=553 ○=554 ◀=935 ╱╱=469 T=320 Ø=368
●=369

⊞=347   ⧄=3328   ⬤=760   △=761   ✕=3046   ◀=208   ⋀=209   ⦰=210   ▢=211   ◯=3011   ⟋=3012
ⴸ=3013   ■=310   ⊡=WHITE

●=744 X=3031 X=553 ✚=554 ⬗=718 ⬗=602 ℓ=601 ◉=935 ─=3348 ╱=320 L=832
O=987 ▲=792 △=793 T=794 •=WHITE

●=900 ◐=947 ○=725 ✛=741 ◎=400 ╱=704 ✕=832

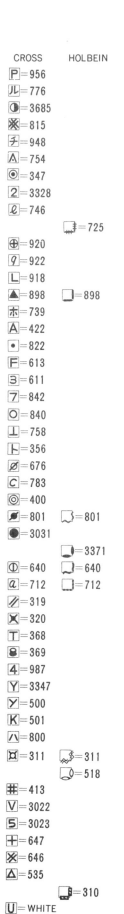

CROSS   HOLBEIN

P = 956
JL = 776
◐ = 3685
※ = 815
ヂ = 948
Λ = 754
◉ = 347
2 = 3328
ℓ = 746
       ▭ = 725
⊕ = 920
9 = 922
L = 918
▲ = 898   ▭ = 898
ホ = 739
Ā = 422
• = 822
F = 613
Ɜ = 611
7 = 842
O = 840
⊥ = 758
Ⱶ = 356
∅ = 676
C = 783
◎ = 400
▰ = 801   ▭ = 801
● = 3031
       ▭ = 3371
Φ = 640   ▭ = 640
ɑ = 712   ▭ = 712
⫽ = 319
✕ = 320
T = 368
ठ = 369
4 = 987
Y = 3347
Ȳ = 500
K = 501
Λ = 800
⋈ = 311   ⌇ = 311
       ▭ = 518
♯ = 413
V = 3022
5 = 3023
+ = 647
✕ = 646
△ = 535
       ▭ = 310
U = WHITE

needlework on page   39

✕ = 824   ▭ = 824 (HOLBEIN)

X = 3685   ☐ = 3685(HOLBEIN)

CROSS	HOLBEIN
‖ = 818	
△ = 776	
▲ = 3689	
⊤ = 891	
⁄ = 894	
B = 350	
T = 352	
● = 498	
◎ = 321	
4 = 741	
⊢ = 744	
✚ = 554	
✕ = 642	
◆ = 920	
Y = 434	
7 = 437	
C = 355	
A = 976	
◢ = 3371	☐ = 3371
K = 801	☐ = 801
◎ = 433	
• = 469	
✕ = 471	
O = 472	
◑ = 987	☐ = 987
% = 470	
⊤ = 905	
⊕ = 703	
⁄ = 704	
a = 367	
V = 320	
⌀ = 368	
5 = 831	
L = 833	
I = 3347	
Y = 3348	
✕ = 935	
2 = 369	
⊞ = 937	
P = 895	
⬤ = 501	
U = 992	
q = 993	
◆ = 500	☐$ = 500
◪ = 807	
b = 334	
◢ = 775	
∃ = 927	
ℓ = 646	
■ = 413	

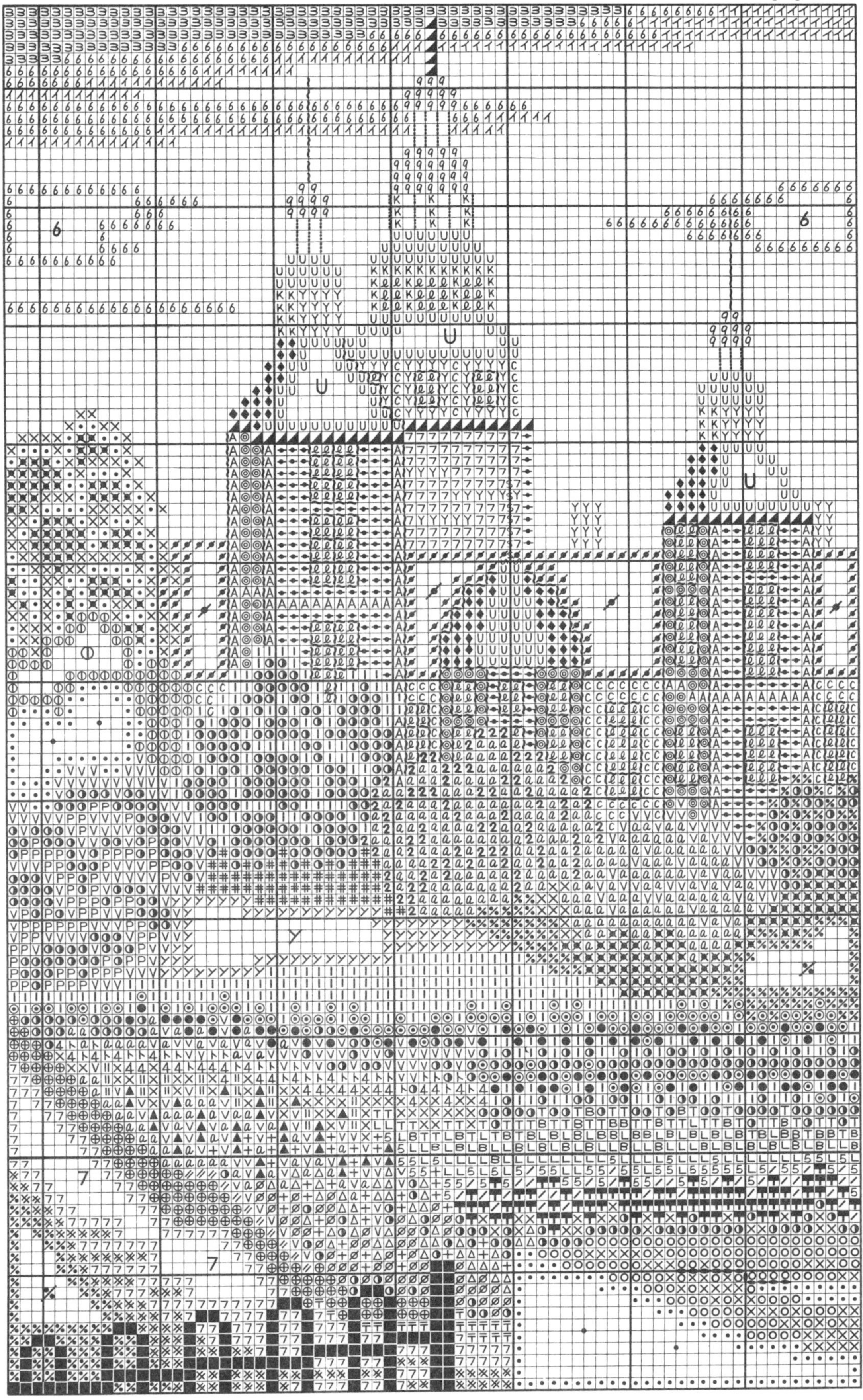

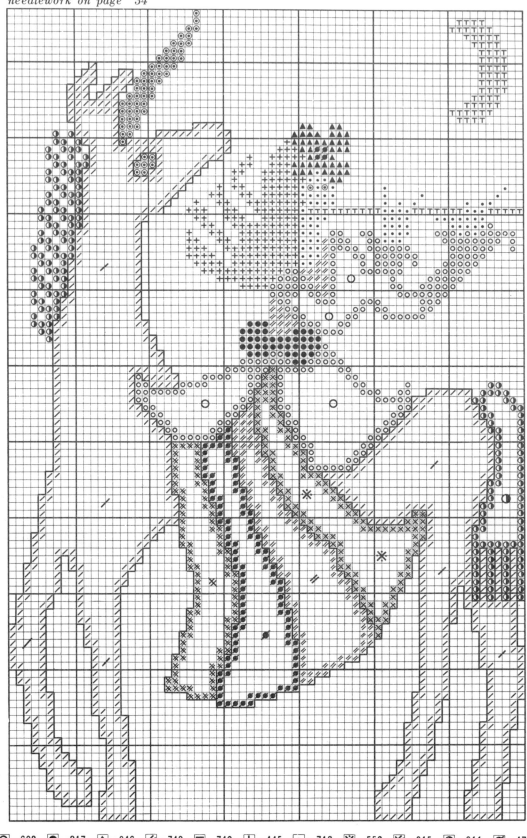

⊙=603 ●=817 ▲=946 ⊘=740 T=742 ✛=445 •=712 ✖=552 ✖=915 ◐=911 ⊘=471
⊙=995 ⁄=WHITE

△=816 ⑦=3354 ✚=3687 ⊕=602 ⊞=600 Ⅴ=712 Ⓢ=975 ⊞=3046 Ⓣ=977 ╱=316 Ⓞ=553
◎=552 ═=915 ▲=3348 ✖=833 ▣=3347 ◣=470 ☒=924 ⊤=806 ╱=318 ·|·=414 ●=310
•=WHITE

⊠=900　△=605　O=977　●=552　L=718　■=211　∧=703　⊠=700　∕=797

●=321 △=605 ◎=742 ☒=783 ☒=729 ■=208 □=718 ☒=700 L=469 ☒=472 O=797

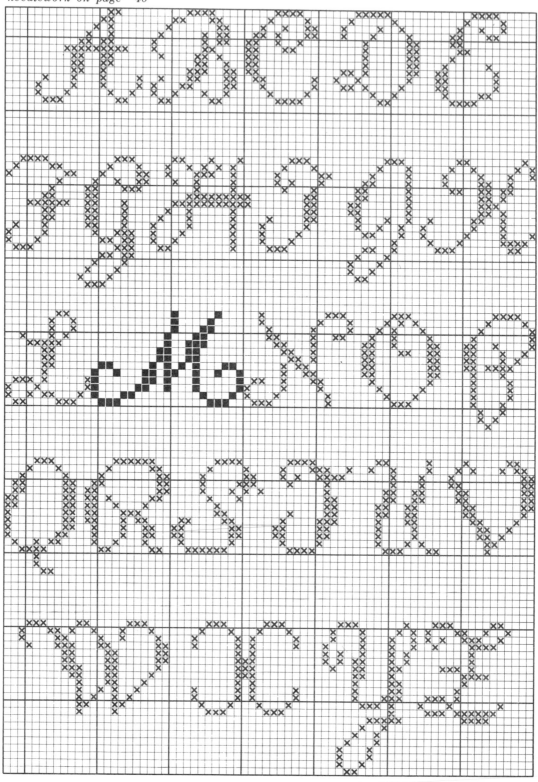

A = 608   B = 740   C = 743   D = 744   E = 995   F = 996   G = 909   H = 911   I = 966   J = 915   K = 917

L = 718   M = 605   N = 3072   O = 415   P = WHITE   Q = 797   R = 798   S = 799   T = 800   U = 550

V = 552   W = 553   X = 666   Y = 891   Z = 957

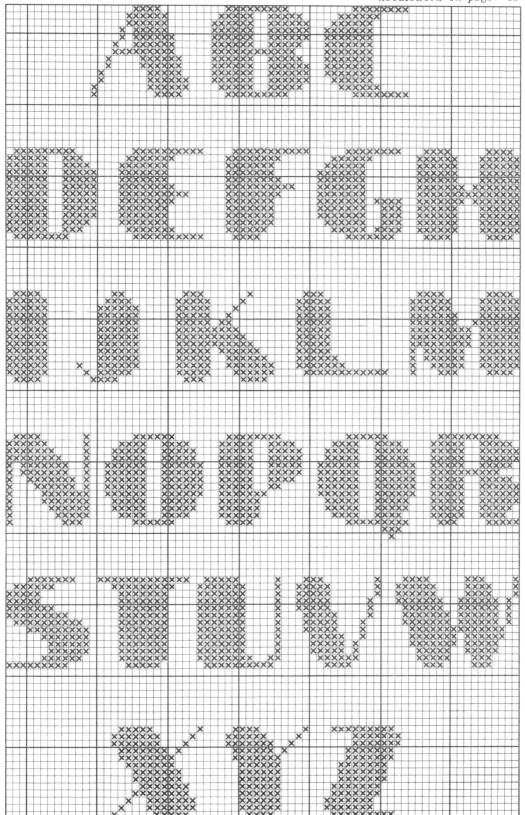

A —304   B = 911   C = 741   D = 987   E = 726   F = 995   G = 552   H = 600   I = 3326   J = 718   K = 640

L = WHITE   M = 445   N = 608   O = 943   P = 816   Q = 893   R = 796   S = 996   T = 3350   U = 208

V = 977   W = 666   X = 601   Y = 992   Z = 704

= =900 ■=608 T=309 +=970 ⊠=444 ✕=919 ●=402 |=976 ∅=550 ⊘=553 ▲=907
⟋=996 ⟋=798 ∧=598 ⊢=924 ◎=930 O=453 —=451

▥=817	☒=352	●=946	∟=309	∨=891	∅=893	○=444	⊰=455	═=725	‖=740	▨=741
▯=746	▰=975	•=680	✛=840	╱=407	▮=838	◡=838(HOLBEIN)	⊥=676	▲=436	△=907	
✳=701	◡=701(HOLBEIN)	▽=702	⬩=704	⋂=732	⊰=733	▢=470				

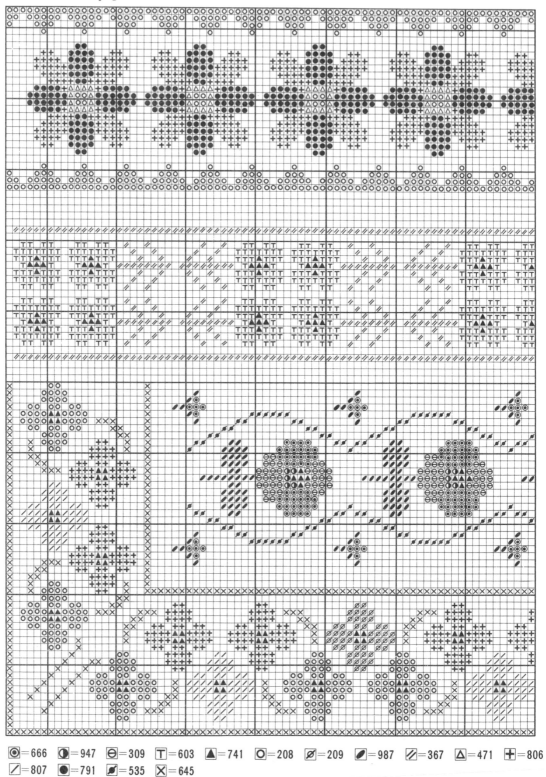

⊙=666 ◑=947 ⊖=309 T=603 ▲=741 O=208 ⊘=209 ✦=987 ⊘=367 △=471 ✚=806

⊘=807 ●=791 ✦=535 ✕=645

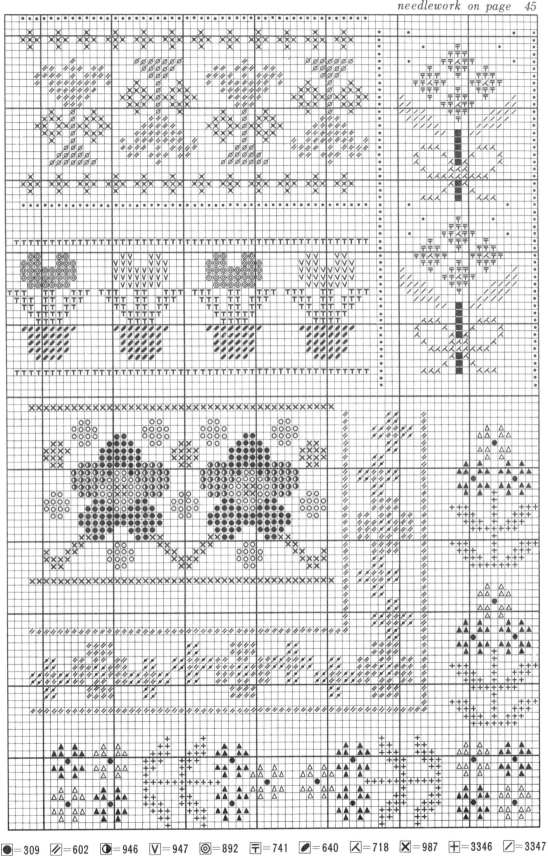

●=309 ⊘=602 ◐=946 Ⅴ=947 ◎=892 ⊤=741 ●=640 人=718 ✕=987 ➕=3346 ◢=3347

◢=470 ◯=833 ⊤=367 ✖=703 ▲=797 △=798 •=535 ⊘=645 ■=3023

◉=817 ◢=900 ◖=815 L=321 ╱=957 ○=977 ◤=915 ●=917 ∧=718 ◗=550 ➕=312

‖=208 ▲=939 T=336 ✕=517

△=347　◨=347(HALF CROSS)　Z=600　C=742　+=740　X=725　◨=725(HALF CROSS)　V=435
◨=435(HALF CROSS)　F=632　●=783　A=301　==976　■=3371　◨=3371(HALF CROSS)
◡=3371(HOLBEIN)　L=718　□=553　▲=550　※=3347　⊢=470　◎=703　O=992
◨=992(HALF CROSS)　◑=799　✖=995　<=996　∥=825　⅄=796

▲=900　△=608　⦶=740　◢=600　◉=603　⊕=606　○=444　Ｉ=742　Λ=307　Ⅲ=445　⊠=640

⧄=977　Ø=839　╱=922　◡=3046(HOLBEIN)　✖=911　T̄=3012　◑=905　T=704　🖊=943

✛=912　●=796　✕=995　◎=793　L=996　■=310　◡=310(HOLBEIN)　◦=WHITE